MW01710734

you a personal question?

Jonny Steele was born a hopeless dancer in Staffordshire, UK. He revelled in the freedom he was allowed as a child, school being the only real annoyance. A decade of turbulent but colourful times followed, as he roamed around on a wing and a prayer.

Jonny has moved house twenty-five times (at last count). He came to Australia to house-sit for three months and found that it more than met his requirements – sun, sand, sport, pretty girls and ice-cold beer. Life's sweet.

Can I ask you a personal question?

JONNY STEELE

PENGUIN BOOKS

PENGUIN BOOKS

Published by the Penguin Group
Penguin Group (Australia)
250 Camberwell Road, Camberwell, Victoria 3124, Australia
(a division of Pearson Australia Group Pty Ltd)
Penguin Group (USA) Inc.
375 Hudson Street, New York, New York 10014, USA
Penguin Group (Canada)
10 Alcorn Avenue, Toronto, Ontario, Canada M4V 3B2
(a division of Pearson Penguin Canada Inc.)
Penguin Books Ltd
80 Strand, London WC2R 0RL, England
Penguin Ireland
25 St Stephen's Green, Dublin 2, Ireland
(a division of Penguin Books Ltd)
Penguin Books India Pvt Ltd
11 Community Centre, Panchsheel Park, New Delhi – 110 017, India
Penguin Group (NZ)
Cnr Airborne and Rosedale Roads, Albany, Auckland, New Zealand
(a division of Pearson New Zealand Ltd)
Penguin Books (South Africa) (Pty) Ltd
24 Sturdee Avenue, Rosebank, Johannesburg 2196, South Africa

Penguin Books Ltd, Registered Offices: 80 Strand, London, WC2R 0RL, England

First published by Penguin Group (Australia), a division of Pearson Australia Group Pty Ltd, 2004

10 9 8 7 6 5 4 3 2 1

Design by Lynn Twelftree © Penguin Group (Australia)
Typeset in Bell Gothic Bold by Midland Typesetters, Maryborough, Victoria
Printed and bound in Australia by McPherson's Printing Group, Maryborough, Victoria

National Library of Australia
Cataloguing-in-Publication data:
Steele, Jonny.
Can I ask you a personal question?

ISBN 0 14 300271 6.

1. Questions and answers. I. Title.

793.73

www.penguin.com.au

Acknowledgements

There are some people I have to thank. We have shared some amazing times together. It has been quite a trip so far. This galaxy of stars includes:

Mom, Dad, Jane, Glenn, my nephew and niece, Pat, Ang, Roger, Ian, Mark and Sarah, Raquel, Macca, Jonty, James, Shelly (a yow), Rik, Mitch, Scott, Barry, Sheila, Deb, Howard, Russ, Clive and Jackie, Pav and Joanna, Jane 11, Bronwyn, all at number 12, Angela, Lyndel, Scratch, and everybody from the glory years at the Nag's Head, Burntwood.

Some fond memories and places of note:

Brownhills, Burntwood, Lichfield, Torquay, Brixton, Surbiton and Cronulla.

Thanks for everything.

Jonny Steele

Introduction

Every day we ask each other questions. The questions we ask don't usually warrant a second thought. We ask and answer them as part of our daily lives.

The questions in this book were written in a light-hearted manner, although some will evoke a more serious response. They will make you laugh and they will rekindle memories of times gone by.

Can I ask you a personal question? is entertaining to read on your own. However, it takes on a new dimension when the questions are asked between two or more people. There are numerous ways to play, but to get started, a tried-and-tested way to 'grill' each other is to ask ten questions then take your turn to answer ten.

This book will tell you something more about yourself and the people you share it with. I hope you enjoy it. Remember – everybody has a past, even you ...

RULES

There are only two rules to follow:

1

You cannot refuse to answer a question

2

You must tell the truth

Only ten questions are on view in order to prevent the person asking them from seeing the following ten questions in advance and 'preparing' an answer to any one of them. This applies when two or more people are taking turns asking each other ten questions at a time.

1

When did you last drink Champagne

2

Have you ever been in an ambulance

3

What are you looking forward to at the moment

4

Are you in touch with any ex-partners

5

Have you or would you ever use a dating service

6

Is there someone you think about every day

7

Have you ever broken into anywhere

8

What do you do when you want to impress someone

9

Who last told you that they love you

10

Do you think you are easy to live with

11

Have you ever taken ecstasy

12

When and where did you last have
a physical fight
Who won

13

How are you in lifts (elevators)

14

Is sex overrated

15

Have you ever thrown up into something not
normally used for that purpose

16

Have you ever inherited any money

17

Do you consider yourself to be a good kisser

18

Who is the nicest person you know

19

What was your last purchase from the chemist

20

How do you prepare your toilet paper for use
(e.g. fold, scrunch)

21

When was the last time you had to apologise

22

What is the first thing you notice when you meet someone

23

Have you ever wet yourself during adulthood

24

What do you wear to look sexy

25

Which political figure have you admired

26

Who do you miss

27

Are you horny when you wake up in the morning

28

How was your skin as a teenager

29

Do you believe in astrology

30

When was the last time you stayed in bed all day

31

Do you buy from charity stores

32

Have you ever walked into the wrong side of a public toilet

33

Who's your best friend

34

Do you have a 'type' (i.e. a specific kind of partner) that you go for

35

What was your first job

36

When was the last time you had a nosebleed

37

Who owes you money

38

Have you ever seen a porn movie

39

Someone is having an epileptic fit –
do you know what to do

40

Are you houseproud

41

What question would you ask the Prime Minister

42

In which class of society do you see yourself

43

Have you ever spent the night in a police cell

44

How fresh is your breath

45

Could you cope as a single parent

46

Do you take notice of the weather forecast

47

When was the last time someone gave you flowers

48

Have you ever asked for a pay rise

49

How do you indulge yourself

50

Is your glass half-empty or half-full

51

What were you doing when you heard that Princess Diana had died

52

What work needs doing to your home

53

Are you ticklish

54

How well do you take criticism

55

Which sporting event do you fantasise about winning

56

Have you ever fallen asleep in the bath

57

Is your signature legible

58

Who's the most awful driver you know

59

What qualifications do you have

60

Are you happy with your speaking voice

61

Have you crossed the equator

62

Which film makes you cry

63

Have you ever witnessed a terrible accident

64

When did you last need the services of a lawyer

65

How often do you get drunk

66

When did you make a fool of yourself

67

What one question would you ask God

68

Do you know of anyone who hates you

69

Should euthanasia be legalised

70

Have you ever been waterskiing

71

Do you envy anybody you know

72

As a child or teenager, which posters were on your wall

73

When were you last nervous

74

Is there a song which always reminds you of someone

75

Whose was the last funeral you attended

76

How would you describe your hair at sixteen

77

How many people always send you a birthday card

78

How much money do you have in the bank

79

Who do you know whose beauty is only skin-deep

80

Do you think anyone fancies you at the moment

81

What's the biggest risk you've ever taken

82

What is your view on nuclear power

83

Can you name a sexy scene in a film

84

What's the most expensive drink you've ever bought

85

What have you argued over with flatmates

86

Do you watch *The Simpsons*

87

Are you comfortable in a high-class restaurant

88

When were you inappropriately dressed

89

Do you have a pet name for your private parts

90

Have you ever received a reward

91

Where did you last have sex

92

How do you relieve stress

93

What annoys you most about people

94

Where was the first place you flew to

95

Have you ever sleepwalked

96

Have you ever had to dial an emergency service

97

Which of your friends would you be happy to date

98

Have you ever fallen down stairs

99

Are you tight with your money

100

Do you get ill often

101

Have you ever had your name in the paper

102

When was the last time you used a laundromat

103

Do you break wind in front of people you know

104

Who do you know without any dress sense

105

What would be your ideal Christmas
And what do you think you'll actually be doing
this year

106
Is your diet important to you

107
Have you got any scars

108
When do you wish you hadn't laughed

109
What's the worst present you've ever been given

110
How much do you owe on your home

111

Who has beautiful eyes

112

What was the first film you ever saw at the cinema

113

Have you ever heard other people making love

114

Have you ever been to a high-school reunion

115

What are you wearing that wasn't fresh on this morning

116

How are your teeth

117

What's the least amount of money you would accept to have sex with someone you detested

118

Are you good at remembering special occasions

119

Do you carry condoms

120

When was the last time you were pressured into doing something

121

Would you refuse to date someone because of their religion

122

What's the biggest mistake you've ever made

123

What products do you keep in your bathroom

124

Are there any compromising photos of you, that you know of

125

Have you ever used a chat-up line

126

Do you talk to yourself

127

When was the last time you pretended to be out

128

Name someone who's always good company

129

Who will be the main beneficiary of your will

130

What are you like when you're drunk

131

How many times have you been in love

132

Has your life ever been in danger

133

Can you play chess

134

Where do you buy your clothes

135

Have you ever been approached
in a public toilet

136

Which historic event do you wish you had witnessed

137

What do you spend most of your money on

138

Do you enjoy giving head

139

When someone pushes in, do you say anything to them

140

Have you ever had an AIDS test

141

How often do you have sex
Is it enough

142

What do you think you'll be like aged 65

143

When talking to others, how do you refer to your partner

144

What did you beg your parents to buy for you

145

Do you wear slippers

146

How often do you get your hair cut

147

Have you ever been on a blind date

148

What's the nicest thing anyone's ever said to you

149

Do you ever worry about the size of your vitals

150

When was the last time someone took you out for a meal

151

When did you last have a flat tyre

152

Do you close your eyes when you kiss

153

Who would you never work with again

154

Have you ever lost a pet

155

Is there anything that all your lovers have had in common

156

Have you ever had sex with a work colleague

157

Do you play the lottery

158

Do you fancy your best friend's partner

159

Which foods can't you stomach

160

Have you ever shat outdoors

161

Would you marry someone your parents disapproved of

162

Have you ever responded to a chain letter

163

When did you last swim in the ocean

164

What's your most treasured possession

165

Who's the most attractive person you've ever had sex with

166

What do you expect from people

167

What was the first CD/record you ever bought

168

Have you ever taken Valium

169

Which country would you most like to visit

170

What's the best thing that's happened today

171

You're going on a long journey – what do you take to occupy yourself

172

What's your favourite sandwich

173

When were you in most pain

174

What was the last card you received that wasn't for Christmas or birthday

175

Do you drop rubbish

176

What do you consider to be sexy

177

Why did you last cry

178

Have you ever had to undergo an initiation ceremony

179

Are you afraid of the dark

180

Would you have sex to advance your career

181

What do you think of students

182

When did you last panic

183

Who did you last write a letter to

184

What's the worst job you've ever had

185

Can you name a product that doesn't do what it says it should

186

Would you consider cosmetic surgery

187

How do you get on with your bank manager

188

Have you kept a letter from an ex-partner

189

Have you ever gone out with your fly undone/ skirt tucked into your knickers

190

Do you have any birthmarks

191

How could your partner improve their body

192

Are you a summer or a winter person

193

Have you ever gone through someone else's possessions

194

Who do you know who's all brains but no sense

195

When do you pay your bills

196

What are you looking forward to today

197

When, where and to whom did you lose your virginity

198

If you could have something named after you, what would you choose

199

Do you live for today or see things in the long term

200

What is the date today

201

Have you ever tried writing a book

202

Who was your best friend at school

203

What did you wear to the last fancy-dress party you went to

204

How old are you

205

Do you look in your hanky after blowing your nose

206

What do you think of Madonna

207

Do you use any sex toys

208

What question would you ask a fortune teller

209

When was the last time you saw someone full-frontal naked

210

As we speak, is there a soft toy on your bed

211

Have you ever been stung by a bee or a wasp

212

Have you ever had an argument
in a public place

213

Do you swear in front of your parents

214

How many continents have you had sex on

215

Do you ever wish you were a different height

216

Which film scares you most

217

When was the last time you were at the zoo

218

Do you take pride in your appearance

219

Are you happy with where you live

220

What do you regret

221

What's the clumsiest pass anyone has ever made at you

222

Have you ever had an electric shock

223

One night of passion, no questions, no strings – who would you choose

224

Have you ever thrown a party

225

When you were a child, did you have an imaginary friend

226

What's your favourite CD at the moment

227

Without looking, how much cash have you got on you

228

Have you ever eaten sushi

229

What do you do on a Sunday morning

230

Have you ever won anything on the lottery

231

Who was the last person to give you a hickey

232

What are your chances of ever needing psychiatric care

233

Can you keep a secret

234

Would it bother you to have a child out of wedlock

235

Silver or gold

236

What's your favourite journey

237

Have you ever mooned or flashed

238

Have you ever fallen over in a bar

239

Who do you consider to be an absolute star

240

Were you ever teacher's pet

241

Can you describe the first time you bought condoms

242

Have you ever been involved in a road accident

243

What award or trophy would you most like to win

244

Which physical feature do you most dislike about yourself

245

Have you ever hitchhiked

246

Does your heart rule your head

247

Has anyone ever peed on you

248

Is there anything in your closet that you bought but have never worn

249

Did your parents smack you

250

Has your current partner met any of your previous ones

251

Have you ever had head lice

252

When was the last time your partner embarrassed you

253

What one thing would you like to change about your home country

254

Someone has been electrocuted – do you know what to do

255

Has a stranger ever helped you out

256

Is there a TV in your bedroom

257

Do you carry an organ donor card

258

What's the worst item in your wardrobe

259

If you had a sex change, what would your name be

260

Can you rollerblade

261

When did you last cringe about something you had done

262

Do you own any family heirlooms

263

What are you particularly good at

264

Can you handle yourself in a fight

265

Who is the funniest person you know

266

Which unusual pet would you like to own

267

When did you last tell someone you loved them

268

Do you have a favourite member of the Royal Family

269

Which is your best side

270

What's the limit on your credit card

271

What do you buy at the duty-free shop

272

What makes you angry

273

When did you last vomit

274

The Beatles or The Stones

275

Whose phone numbers do you know by heart

276

Were you a happy teenager

277

You're alone at home lounging about – what are you wearing

278

Who gets on your nerves

Why

279

Do you have any inhibitions when it comes to sex

280

Do you always carry a pen

281

A loved one loses an arm in an accident – do you go back and get the limb

282

Which musical instrument/s did you learn at school

283

Whose was the last wedding you attended

284

What are you obsessed with

285

What's your favourite sound

286

When was the last time you were dumped

287

What's your party piece

288

When did you last cheat at a game

289

How often do you vacuum

290

How's your posture

291

Are you patriotic

292

Considering your current lifestyle, how long do you think you'll live

293

What are you particularly hopeless at

294

Have you ever had to use something other than toilet paper

295

What's the least amount of money you could survive on for a week

296

Who has a great voice

297

What happened on your formal night

298

What's the longest period you've gone without sex

299

When did you last hold a baby

300

Would you go out with someone boring simply because of their looks

301

What was the last item you bought at sale price

302

How many school friends are you still in contact with

303

Describe your last job interview

304

How do you get on with your brothers/sisters

305

Do you own anything with diamonds

306

Have you ever called a partner by the wrong name

307

Have you ever fallen over in a public place

308

Do you believe in UFOs

309

Which member of your family do you try to avoid

310

Dogs or cats

311

Who's your hero

312

How do you eat a banana

313

What's your earliest memory

314

Have you ever broken a mirror

315

What's the sexiest thing someone has said to you

316

If you were a product-tester, what product would it be

317

Were you ever a member of a fan club

318

Can you ski

319

Have you ever been tied up during sex

320

Can you name a present you got the Christmas before last

321

Are you punctual

322

Is there anything under your pillow

323

Which job would you never do

324

What do you think about

325

How do you cure hiccups

326

What day of your life would you happily re-live

327

Who would you be in *Friends*

328

How many people have you had sex with

329

Do you think you're ready to move house

330

How much pocket money were you given as a child

331

Whose company do you find boring

332

What embarrasses you

333

Where's the most unusual place you've had sex

334

Have you ever been camping

335

When did you last go to church

336
Can you roll your tongue

337
Which household item are you about to run out of

338
It's your turn to karaoke – what's the song

339
Who last cooked a meal for you

340
What was the first R-rated film you saw
How old were you

341

Burial or cremation

342

Have you ever used food during sex

343

Would you have a long engagement

344

Do you get travel-sick

345

Have you ever been scuba diving

346

Do you have any recurring dreams

347

Have you ever been burgled

348

What was the last competition you entered

349

Have you ever seen a ghost

350

Would you consider an orgy

351

What four things would be on your coat of arms

352

Who do you owe money to

353

Have you ever said 'I love you' without meaning it

354

Which character would you love to play on stage or screen

355

Have you ever watched a porn movie with a partner

356

Which is your most uncomfortable piece of clothing

357

Can you use chopsticks

358

Should prostitution be legalised

359

Have you ever gatecrashed a party

360

What's the longest period you've been unemployed

361

What's your blood type

362

What song is guaranteed to get you on the dance floor

363

How would you sum up your life so far

364

Do you carry a hanky

365

Which part of your body last sported a bandaid

366

Would you send your children to a private school

367

How do you refer to a penis

368

Would you ever hire a prostitute

369

What are your neighbours like

370

When did you last tell a lie

371

Have you ever been fired

372

Are you allergic to anything

373

When did you last talk to a priest

374

Have you ever been two-timed
How did you find out

375

What one thing would improve the
quality of your life

376

How long does it take you to sew on a button

377

Do you believe in the Loch Ness Monster

378

Does religion play a major part in your life

379

How will you be voting in the next election

380

Do you think men and women can be good friends without sex getting in the way

381

Have you ever locked yourself out

382

When did you last ride in a taxi

383

How many valentine cards did you get this year

384

How many valentine cards did you send this year

385

When did you come closest to death

386
What was the last thing you borrowed

387
Have you ever used a bidet

388
What turns you off

389
Are you comfortable in the company of gay people

390
What's the best book you've ever read

391

Can you describe any experience you've had with drugs

392

Have you had any operations

393

What do you do after sex

394

When did you last claim insurance

395

Were you ever bullied

396

Have you had a holiday fling

397

At what time do you normally go to bed

398

Have you ever forged someone's signature

399

Why did you last talk to a police officer

400

How did you discover the facts of life

401

Are you a godparent

402

You have a month to live – how do you spend the time

403

Have you ever driven drunk

404

How do you like your steak cooked

405

Have you ever dressed up during sex

406

What's the lowest monthly wage you would work for

407

Have you ever broken a window

408

When did you last have a black eye

409

Who don't you trust

410

What's been the best day of your life so far

411

What's the tallest building you've been up

412

Have you ever had a sexually transmitted disease

413

What have you won in competitions or prize draws

414

Can you change a nappy

415

Spectacles or contact lenses

416

Has anyone ever lost their virginity to you

417

How are your table manners

418

Have you ever had a long-distance relationship

419

What makes you cry

420

Would you take a parachute jump

421

Do you fancy the idea of three in a bed

422

Do you pray

423

Have you ever had sex with someone you had no feelings for

424

How many of the Seven Dwarfs can you name

425

Have you ever fallen asleep at the dinner table

426

What's your favourite cheese

427

How are you on the dance floor

428

When were you caught red-handed

429

Is there someone you worry about

430

Which TV programs do you avoid missing at all costs

431

Who was your favourite teacher

432

Who (living or dead) would you most like to meet

433

How many sexual partners did you have last year

434

Someone is choking – do you know what to do

435

Do you enjoy Guinness

436

What's your favourite salad dressing

437

Are you a moody person

438

What do you shave

439

Who's the worst boss you've worked for

440

Have you ever faked an orgasm

441

Have you ever been in close proximity to someone really famous

442

What do you do when you get a cold

443

Have you ever broken your word

444

What's your greatest fear

445

You have to join up – which one of the armed forces do you choose

446

Do you have any autographs

447

How are you on aeroplanes

448

Since childhood, have you ever had to wear a uniform

449

Can you tell me how much petrol costs, per litre

450

Do you suspect any of your friends to be gay

451

Where is the worst place you've ever slept?

452

Do you bite your nails

453

When was the last time you stayed
up for twenty-four hours

454

Do you play gambling machines

455

Do you believe in love at first sight

456

When do you wish you hadn't cried

457

Are you popular at work

458

Do you know all the words to your national anthem

459

Have you kept any press cuttings

460

Have you ever sunbathed nude

461

When did you last have to borrow money

462

What's the greatest distance you've ever travelled alone

463

Describe your earliest sexual experience

464

Have you eaten squid or octopus

465

Which cartoon character most resembles you

466

When did you last put your foot in it

467

Is there someone you know who you feel sorry for

468

Can you tell your favourite ioke

469

What's your cure for a hangover

470

What was the last thing you bought from a vending machine

471

What do you keep your photographs in

472

How would you choose to die

473

Have you ever been involved in a protest march or demonstration

474

Do you know a drug addict

475

Are you any good at pool

476

What have you got that's hidden

477

What's your all-time favourite meal

478

Have you ever made an anonymous phone call

479

Do you know your inside-leg measurement

480

Do you have any superstitious rituals

481

What do you call your parents

482

Someone is drunk – what word do you use to describe their state

483

Have you ever two-timed
If so, did you own up or were you caught

484

Should pornography be banned

485

What was the last thing you lost

486

Do you prefer to be on top during sex

487

Have you ever drunk ouzo

488

Do you have anything pierced

489

Have you ever been unconscious

490

Can you recite the message on your answering machine

491

How do you like your eggs

492

Which animal would you like to be

493

When was the last time you sang 'Happy Birthday'

494

Are you going to heaven

495

Who broke your heart

496

It's cocktail hour – what's your pick

497

Which teacher had it in for you

498

When was the last time you broke the law

499

Who do you admire

500

Have you ever seen a dead body

501

Which CD in your collection do you never play

502

Coke or Pepsi

503

Who's the ugliest person you know

504

Have you ever dressed up as a member of the opposite sex

505

What do you wear to bed

506

Do you put the milk in before or after removing the tea bag

507

Would you date me if I asked you

508

Would you die for anyone

509

Do you keep a diary

510

What's the most beautiful building you've ever seen

511

Do you dream in colour

512

What's your favourite soup

513

What would you say to the Pope

514

Which would you rather lose – your hair or your teeth

515

Are you a morning or a night person

516

What are your thoughts on the meaning of life

517

Do you have any toilet rituals

518

What is your nightmare date

519

Does screen violence lead to real violence

520

What is your favourite quotation

521

Have you accidentally injured anyone

522

Which nationality, other than your own, would you like to be

523

Can you do any accents

524

Do you consider yourself to be attractive

525

What was the last thing you were promised

526

Have you ever been stood up

527

What reading matter is currently by your bed

528

Are you happy with your nose

529

Do you keep in touch

530

Are you computer-literate

531

Have you ever worn a wig

532

Have you ever appeared in court

533

Which musical instrument do you wish you could play

534

Who's the most gorgeous person you've been in the same room with

535

Have you ever had a credit card refused

536

Do you wear any hats

537

What's your favourite pasta dish

538

Do you tan easily

539

What's under your bed

540

What's the cruelest thing you've ever done

541

How would you hate to die

542

Have you ever ridden a horse

543

Should marijuana be legalised

544

Which three songs would you like played at your funeral

545

How quickly do you fall in love

546

Do you know any card tricks

547

Are you afraid of heights

548

Would you date someone whose political views were opposite to yours

549

Are you addicted to anything

550

Have you broken any of your bones

551

You win the lottery – what's your first purchase

552

Can you sleep with the light on

553

Have you ever found out too late that there's no toilet paper

554

Are you vain

555

Do you believe in marriage

556

Do you live to work or work to live

557

Have you eaten frogs' legs

558

Was there ever anyone more in love with you than vice versa

559

Do you know anyone who is left-handed

560

When were you at your physical peak

561

Can you name a dreadful record

562

Are you happy with your passport photo

563

Do you keep promises

564

Have you ever sent a fan letter to anyone

Did you receive a reply

565

Are you tactile

566

Have you ever sent a meal back to the kitchen in a restaurant

567

Have you done someone a good turn

568

Have you ever had a nude sauna

569

Have you kept your New Year's resolutions so far this year

570

What's your current nickname

571

How would you like you or your partner to give birth

572

Which soap operas do you watch

573

Who do you wish you hadn't lost contact with

574

Have you got your own mug or cup

575

Do you sleep easily

576
Did you swear at anybody today

577
Which quiz show would you like to appear on

578
Have you ever gone through customs without declaring something

579
Are you organised

580
Do you always get out of the pool to pee

581

What's on your bedroom wall

582

How do you greet a friend

583

Tell me something you think would surprise people about you

584

Do you get migraines

585

Can you roll a cigarette

586

Can you recite any poetry

587

Are you on any medication at the moment

588

How do you refer to breasts

589

What's the largest amount of money you've held in your hands

590

What's your strongest colour in Trivial Pursuit

591

Do you have any lucky charms

592

How would you describe your handwriting

593

What's the best stage show you've ever seen

594

When was the last time you trod in dog shit

595

What do you believe in

596

How do you like your potatoes cooked

597

How old were you when you left home

598

Are you a big tipper

599

How do you keep up with what's going on in the world

600

Have you ever got a parking fine

601

Which court case would you like to have been a juror on

602

Can you name a person of the same sex who you find attractive

603

Have you ever been to Africa

604

What were you like as a child

605

Have you ever eaten oysters

606

When were you truly gobsmacked

607

When did you last change your toothbrush

608

Have you got a scrapbook

609

What's your middle name

610

Have you ever done the dirty with your best friend's partner

611

Where do you buy your underwear

612

What's the best meal you've ever eaten

613

What will you be doing this New Year's Eve

614

Have you ever completed a cryptic crossword

615

Were you in the school play

616

What kind of driver are you

617

What was the first gig you went to

618

Who should be shot

619

Are you a gossip

620

When was the last time you had diarrhoea

621

Do you wear any jewellery

622

Do you enjoy being the centre of attention

623

What is the ideal number of children to have

624

Which car would you love to own

625

Can you spell – if yes, then spell 'committed'

626

What's your most treasured and irreplaceable possession

627

Who makes you laugh

628

Who was the last person you slept with

629

Do you clip, cut or pick your nails

630

What's in your car stereo at the moment

631

How would you like to be proposed to

632

What's the best advice you've ever received

633

Would you like a tattoo
What design and where

634

If you could change your name,
what would you choose

635

What characteristics have you inherited
from your parents

636

Which actor would play you in a film about your life

637

What do you choose from the wine list

638

Is there one piece of criticism that sticks in your mind

639

Can you describe your ideal night out

640

Do you believe in God

641

Would you consider an open marriage

642

Where was the first place you went on holiday with a lover

643

Have you ever vandalised anything

644

Who's the most intelligent person you know

645

Do you hold grudges

646

What do you think of ballet

647

What will you do when you retire

648

Have you ever been burnt by fire

649

How long does it take you to get ready in the morning

650

Do you squeeze your pimples

651

Are you a member of any clubs

652

What's the funniest film you've ever seen

653

Would you say you were a patient person

654

Have you ever skinny-dipped

655

Michael Jackson – what do you think?

656

What's the nicest thing you've received in the post

657

Can you hold your liquor

658

Who do you telephone most often

659

Do you sleep better on your own

660

What would you spend your last $100 on

661

What's your usual drink in the bar

662

Are you photogenic

663

If anything, what would you change about your personality

664

Which sporting event would you most like tickets for

665

Did you ever run away from home

666
What do you think of Shakespeare

667
Have you ever had sex with a married person

668
What do you have for breakfast

669
Who was your favourite auntie or uncle

670
Which item of clothing do you really need at the moment

671

Are you afraid of death

672

Have you ever shoplifted

673

Who was your first love

674

Have you ever attempted to eat a really hot chilli

675

Have you ever received a telegram

676

Could you ever run a marathon

677

What's been playing on your mind today

678

Are you anti-abortion

679

On which attempt did you pass your driving test

680

How's your maths – you have twenty seconds to tell me what 17 x 13 equals (221)

681

What was the last thing you took back to a shop

682

Have you ever considered suicide

683

Have you ever left a tap on, with dire consequences

684

What makes you blush

685

What do you have on toast

686

Has anything changed about your life this year

687

Who's the coolest person you know

688

For a long journey, what's your preferred mode of transport

689

Does anyone you know intimidate you

690

What's your most pleasant characteristic

691

Have you ever been caught having sex

692

How many gay friends do you have

693

Do you always wash your hands after using the loo

694

Have you ever been prosecuted

695

Which of the five senses would you most hate to lose

696

What ambitions do you still have to fulfil

697

What exercise do you do

698

Have you ever worked abroad

699

You're about to be executed – any last requests

700

What do you think of boxing

701

When did you feel betrayed

702

Have you ever cheated on a partner

703

Can you touch your nose with your tongue

704

Have you ever been somebody's boss
Did you enjoy it

705

With what word do you refer to the act
of having sex

706

What did you enjoy on TV yesterday

707

Who is your favourite writer

708

Are you afraid of failure

709

The dessert trolley has arrived –
what are you having

710

What would your autobiography be called

711

What do you never leave home without

712

Do you talk during sex

713

Do you pray

714

Who are your best male and female friends

715

Which team do you support

716

Can you describe your ideal wedding

717

Who would you most like to meet

718

When you look in the mirror, do you like what you see

719

Are there any illegal substances you'd like to try once

720

Who is the most irritating person you know

721

Would you appear naked in a film or play

722

What would you cook for me if I came round for a meal

723

Are you true to your word

724

Have you ever been mugged

725

What do you think when you see old photos of yourself

726

Can you name a great film

727

How many hours sleep do you need each night

728

Have you ever done a runner without paying

729

When was the last time you shouted at someone

730

Do you have a favourite advertisement

731

Are you good with money

732

Who do you regret having sex with

733

What do you want for Christmas

734

What's in your purse/wallet

735

Can you describe a memory that makes you laugh

736

How many pillows do you sleep on

737

Have you ever paid for a massage

738

When did all your efforts go unappreciated

739

Do you like classical music

740

Are you a hypochondriac

741

If you could be a fly on the wall,
where would you land

742

What do you take into the bath with you

743

Are you a good swimmer

744

Have you ever had food poisoning

745

Do you carry photographs of anyone

746

Can you whistle using your fingers

747

Who's your favourite 007

748

Have you ever smoked

It so, can you describe your first time

749

Whose chat show, past or present,

would you like to appear on

750

What do you think of hunting

751

Have you ever poured a drink over someone's head

752

Do you think about previous partners

753

When do you wish you hadn't broken wind

754

Have you ever brewed your own booze

755

How do you relax

756

Holidays – do you sunbathe or see the sights

757

Do you have a calendar in your home

758

What's your most memorable sexual experience

759

Have you ever slept rough

760

When was the last time you wanted to hit somebody

761

Which shop purchases do you find embarrassing

762

What's the hottest place you've been to

763

Can you name a great actress

764

Can you describe your first kiss

765

What's the most amazing coincidence you've experienced

766

Have you ever had an injection in your backside

767

What's the last thing you do before going to bed

768

What are you dreading about getting old

769

Did you fancy a stranger at any point today

770

Do you use your local library

771

What was your best subject at school

772

Do you have one-night stands

773

Can you name the current number one single

774

When did you last wet the bed

775

Have you ever had to make a speech

776

What are you proud of

777

Which member of your family has caused the most trouble

778

Would you date someone who had a disability

779

When do you do your Christmas shopping

780

You're granted one wish – what's it to be

781

What illegal drugs have you taken

782

Do you walk under ladders

783

What's the largest amount you've written a cheque for

784

What is the part of your body that you most admire

785

Do you use product in your hair

786

Marilyn Monroe – murdered or suicide

787

Have you ever given blood

788

How are you with creepy crawlies

789

Do you like talking about yourself

790

Have you ever walked in on someone having sex

791

What one piece of advice would you give to your children

792

Can you read a map

793

Who's the most famous person you've met

794

Were you ever suspended from high school

795

When was the last time you were turned down after asking someone out on a date

796
What was the last book you bought

797
Do you think about sex every day

798
Could you strip for a living

799
Which position are you most likely to fall asleep in

800
Have you ever eaten lobster

801

Which hair colour would you like to try

802

Have you won any awards

803

Who spoils you

804

Do you ever feel old

805

Something smells terrible – what word do you use to describe it

806

What was the worst day of your life

807

How are you environmentally friendly

808

Which accent do you like

809

You have five words to describe your ideal partner – what are they

810

Have you ever blackmailed anyone (emotionally or otherwise)

811

Has a person of the same sex ever told you they loved you

812

What was the last racist remark you made

813

Have you ever got off with someone at a work party

814

Can you describe your favourite photograph

815

Have you ever been kicked in the crotch

816

What did you want to be when you grew up

817

What did you eat for dinner last night

818

What's your biggest weakness

819

Who do you know personally who's been in prison

820

Have you ever followed anyone

821

Do you know which day of the week you were born

822

Are you sensible

823

Blondes, brunettes or redheads

824

Have you ever been flashed

825

Who do you wish you'd had the chance to meet before they died

826

Can you stand the sight of blood

827

Bath or shower

828

When was the last time you were really under pressure

829

Who did you run to – mum or dad

830

Have you ever dodged a fare on public transport

831

Which of your friends is the most attractive

832

Are you good at telling jokes
Can you tell one now

833

As a child, what was your favourite TV program

834

What's the most romantic thing that's ever been done for you

835

What are you like when you wake up

836

When have you lied about your age

837

Have you ever fainted

838

Who do you know that's completely unreliable

839

Are you scared of needles

840

Can you sing

841

What's the most romantic thing you've ever done for someone

842

What would you do differently if you were ten years younger

843

Who did you last speak to on the telephone

844

Can you mend a fuse

845

When were you at your most drunk

846

Have you ever written graffiti on anything

847

How are you at the dentist

848

Have you ever ridden a motorbike

849

What's your claim to fame

850

Could you put an injured animal out of its misery

851

Have you told a lie today

852

You're off to a desert island – what three things do you take with you

853

Who do you know who smells

854

What's the largest amount of money you would bet on a horse race

855

Can you do any impressions

856

Have you ever bought anything at an auction

857

Do you wear a watch

858

Can you shoot a gun

859

What do you love the smell of

860

When did you last go out with your parents

861

If you could choose any city in the world, where would you visit

862

Can you juggle

863

Do you prefer sweet or savoury

864

What make are your sunglasses

865

When was the last time you were on a boat

866

How do you deal with spiders in your home

867

Have you ever eaten or drunk anything just to be polite

868

Can you speak a foreign language

869

What's your favourite flavour of chips

870

Were you ever promiscuous

871
Have you ever been thrown out of a nightclub

872
Do you know the international dialling code for your home country

873
How do you deal with unwanted salespeople on the phone or at the door

874
Ideally, how many times a week would you like to have sex

875
Would you tell a friend if their breath smelt

876

A good-looking stranger on the beach asks you to rub sunscreen on them – yes or no

877

Do you bring your work home with you

878

What's the fastest you've ever been in a car

879

You see someone being attacked – do you stop and help them

880

Have you been in a hot-air balloon

881

Do you give to beggars on the street

882

How often do you take a shower or bath

883

Do you think space exploration is a waste of money

884

Have you ever taken or come into contact with cocaine

885

Do you ever go out without underwear

886

Have you ever eaten the worm from a bottle of tequila

887

When, if ever, were you ashamed of your country

888

What's your favourite colour

889

If you could bring someone back to life, who would it be

890

Are you happy with your image

891

Are you a member of the Mile High Club

892

Have you ever been on crutches

893

What's your favourite charity to give to

894

Where did you see the most beautiful sunset
Were you alone

895

When did you refuse to have sex

896

When did you show courage

897

How do you reject the offer of a date

898

Do you believe in fate

899

Are you happy with your life at present

900

When did you forgive but not forget

901

Does age bother you when it comes to dating

902

When did you last kiss on a beach, and who

903

Who are you always pleased to see

904

Do you pick your nose every day

905

When did you last visit the doctor
Why

906

How do you rate yourself as a lover, out of ten

907

Who was your last phone call made to and why

908

Do you try not to make a noise when you go to the toilet

909

When did you last gamble, how much did you bet, and did you win

910

Do you floss

911

How much do you weigh

912

What's the most expensive item of clothing you own

913

Have you saved somebody's life

914

Where did you last fly to on your own

915

How often do you get takeaway food delivered home

916

Do you wish the colour of your eyes was different

917

Where did you last take photos

918

Do you own a set of handcuffs
If so, what do you use them for

919

What size are your feet

920

Who do you have the most respect for

921

Who did you last buy a present for

922

Have you ever been rescued

923

Are men and women equal

924

Do you find me attractive

925

Have you ever had sex in the ocean

926

If you could, what would you change about your partner

927

Who is the most attractive person at work

928

Who did you last go to the cinema with

929

What size is your waist

930

Has anyone annoyed you today

931

How could you improve yourself

932

If you were reborn, would you choose to be a man or a woman

933

What is your biggest weakness when it comes to food

934

Have you ever been on TV

935

What's your latest fad

936

Tea or coffee

937

Have you ever paid for sex

938

Do you snore

939

Could you eat another human in order to survive

940

How long before a trip do you pack

941

When did you last get your fortune told, and what was said

942

How would you discipline your child

943

Who do you think is the biggest threat to world peace

944

Do you drink too much alcohol

945

Would you masturbate in front of your partner

946

Who gives you the creeps

947

Do you have any recurring dreams

948

When did you last lose your temper

949

Do you know your way around the body of the opposite sex

950

How would you choose to die

951

Do you believe in life after death

952

What was your last argument about and who was it with

953

What's the best present you've been given and who gave it to you

954

What's the 'furthest' you've been on a first date

955

What do you cook for a romantic dinner

956

What's your ideal occupation

957

On the train, which way do you face

958

Do you own a gun

959

Do you like your partner's family

960

When were you ripped off

961

What would you change if you had your life over again

962

Can violence solve a problem

963

Are you a good masseur/masseuse

964

How much do you pay for a haircut

965

When did you last have breakfast in bed

966

How do you remove unwanted hair

967

Are you happy with your body

968

What's the best hotel you have ever stayed in

969

What was the last item you hired

970

Are you in debt

971

What's the most boring aspect of your life

972

What first attracts you to someone

973

What's the shortest period of time you've had between meeting someone new and having sex with them

974

Are you happy in your own company

975

How often do you clean your ears

976

Would you refuse to date someone because of their occupation

977

Do you always insist on a condom

978

Is there someone you know whose life you'd hate to have

979

Do you judge people on first impressions What do you look for

980

What did you dream about last night

981

What's the most important decision you've ever made

982

Where do you go to be on your own

983

Have you ever run over an animal

984

Are you happy with your butt

985

TV or radio

986

Which newspaper do you read

987

How often do you change the linen on your bed

988

When was your patience last tested

989

Can you name someone you don't trust

990

Who made you laugh today

991

Are you proud of your nationality

992

What's your solution to terrorist attacks

993

What do you want that you can't afford

994

Would you marry someone who asked you to sign a pre-nuptial agreement

995

What colour underwear do you have on

996

Whose company do you try to avoid

997

Are you always ready for sex

998

Love or money

999

Where do you see yourself in ten years

1000

How do you feel about the person who's been asking you these questions